The Story of SALT

The Story of SALT

MARK KURLANSKY — S. D. SCHINDLER

PUFFIN BOOKS
AN IMPRINT OF PENGUIN GROUP (USA)

MY ROCK

It began a few years ago with a rock I bought in a small mountain town in Spain. The rock had pink surfaces with streaks of white and brown. Though it was not a diamond or an emerald or a ruby, it was beautiful. Yet, it was only salt.

I took my rock home and put it on a windowsill. One day it got rained on, and white crystals started appearing on the pink. My beautiful pink rock was starting to look like white salt and that seemed very ordinary. So I rinsed the crystals off the rock with water. Then for fifteen minutes I carefully patted the rock dry with a towel.

When I woke up the next day, the rock was pink again, but it was sitting in a puddle of salt water that had leaked out of it. The sun was heating the water and after a few hours, square white crystals began to appear. This is called solar evaporation and is the exact way that ocean water is turned into salt.

For a while it seemed I had a magical stone that would continually produce salt water. The rock never seemed to get smaller. Sometimes, I thought the rock had completely dried out. But then, on a humid or rainy day, another puddle would appear under it. I decided to experiment and dry the rock out by baking it in a toaster oven. Within a half hour, I saw it had grown stalactites, long thin tentacles of white crystal drooping down from the toaster grill. I brushed them off and my rock looked the same as before.

My rock lived by its own rules.

When friends came over, I would show them the rock and tell them that it was salt. They would always ask to lick it, to see if it was true.

My rock was only salt, which we sprinkle on our food every day without a thought. But that simple common thing—salt, or NaCl, as it is known chemically—has been the object of wars and revolutions. It has fascinated people and preoccupied economies since before recorded history.

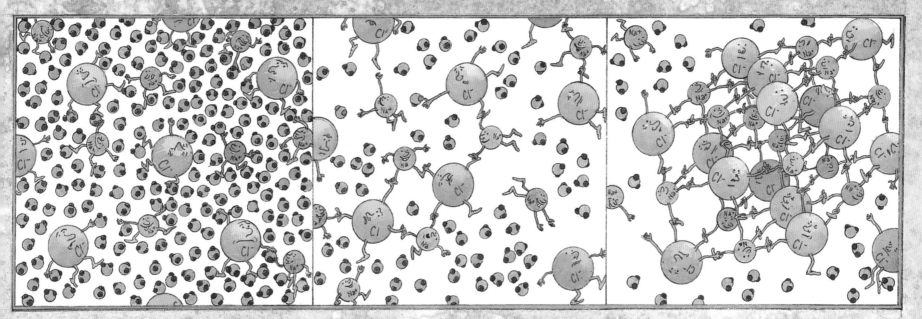

$$Na^+ + Cl^- = Salt!$$

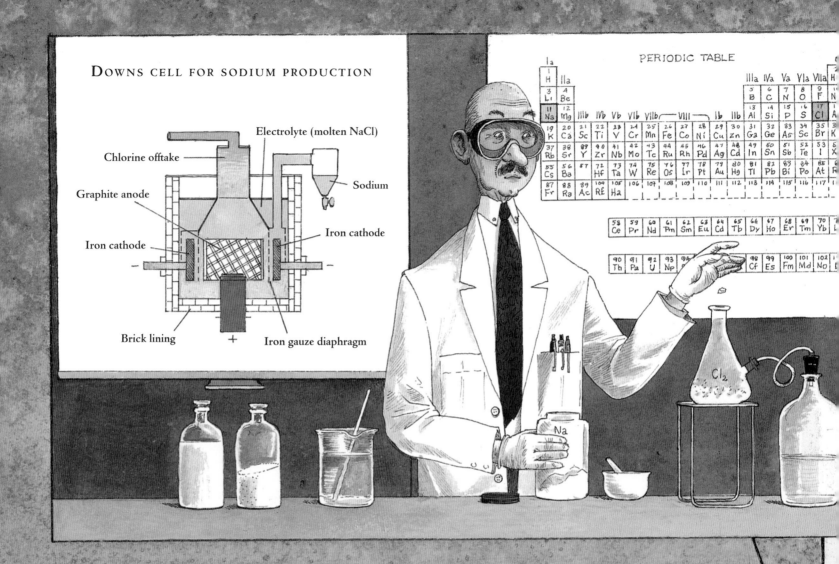

What Is Salt?

The earth is made up of ninety-two natural elements, which combine in nature to form compounds. Salt is a compound produced when sodium (Na^+), a metal so unstable that it easily bursts into flame, combines with chlorine (Cl^-), a deadly poisonous gas. This natural occurrence is known as a chemical reaction—think of it as two people who misbehave on their own but play well together. The two elements stabilize each other, and the resulting compound, sodium chloride, is neither explosive nor poisonous. This is what we call salt.

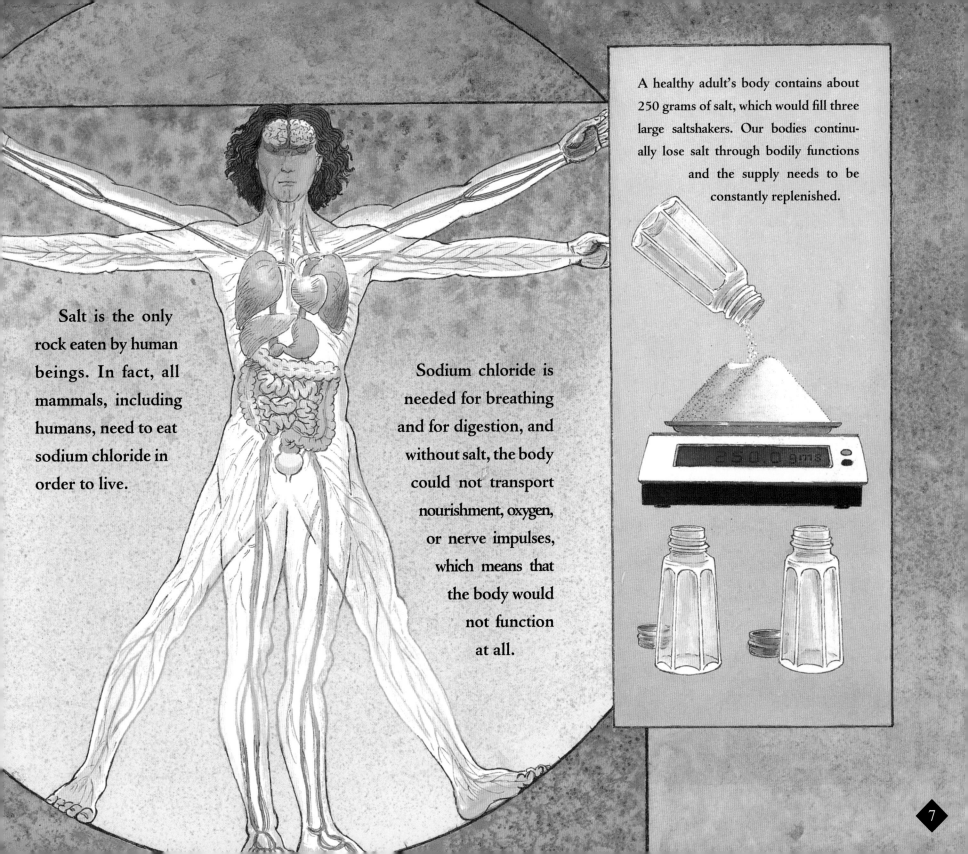

Salt is the only rock eaten by human beings. In fact, all mammals, including humans, need to eat sodium chloride in order to live.

Sodium chloride is needed for breathing and for digestion, and without salt, the body could not transport nourishment, oxygen, or nerve impulses, which means that the body would not function at all.

A healthy adult's body contains about 250 grams of salt, which would fill three large saltshakers. Our bodies continually lose salt through bodily functions and the supply needs to be constantly replenished.

How to Make Salt

The four most common ways to find salt in nature are on the ground in dry salt beds, in the oceans, in underground springs, and in rocks under the earth.

Humans first found salt on the surface of the land, where ancient salt lakes had dried up. Animals, who need even more salt than people, were usually the first to discover these places, sometimes called salt licks because animals would go lick the salty ground. When humans wanted to gather this salt, they simply scraped it up from the ground.

The most plentiful source of salt is the ocean. But seawater must be boiled for many hours before the water has evaporated and only salt is left. This is a very expensive way to produce salt because a great deal of fuel, such as wood or coal, must be burned up. The fuel may be more valuable than the salt.

One solution is to enclose the seawater in man-made ponds at the edge of the ocean and let it heat in the sun. This is a very slow process. The ponds can take more than a year to evaporate to salt crystals. But both the salt and the sunlight are free.

Salt is also found in underwater springs. In 200 B.C., a man named Li Bing, the governor of the Sichuan province in central China, discovered that springs of salty water came from under the earth. Because this water is usually saltier than the ocean, it does not take as much time or fuel to boil it into salt. To get to the springs, the Chinese began drilling into the earth by pounding on long iron chisels. Then, long bamboo tubes were lowered on ropes into the holes to scoop up the salt water.

The work could be dangerous. Some of the workers drilling the holes would get sick. Sometimes flames would spit out of the hole. Occasionally a tremendous explosion would erupt and kill an entire crew. With no other explanation at hand, the people of Sichuan concluded that there were dragons under the earth, guarding the precious salt.

However, by A.D. 100 they came to understand that there was an invisible substance in the holes that would travel up the pipe. The pipe led to the house where the salt water was boiled. The workers learned to light the end of the pipe where the fumes came out to produce a flame that could heat the pots of salt water to boil out the salt. This is the earliest known use of natural gas in the world.

Another source of salt is rocks that are mined under the ground. There are large rock salt deposits in many parts of the United States, including Louisiana and Texas. Rock salt is still mined under Cleveland and Detroit today. Most rock salt is extremely pure.

Once miners turn on the lights, each salt mine looks unique. Some have black or gray walls, and others are so white, they look like a snowstorm just passed through. Some have white stripes while others, such as the mine in Cardona in northern Spain, have brightly colored stripes. Some mines have underground rivers and lakes that can be crossed by boat, and one mine in southern Poland even has ornate rooms carved out of salt!

Wieliczka salt mine 1867

Salting Civilization

Everywhere in the world, it has been found that early humans who survived by eating wild animals and gathering wild edible plants did not have to think about salt. Salt is in the blood and flesh of animals, so hunters got all the salt they needed.

But once people settled in one place and began farming to produce food, they had a great need for salt. Eating vegetables and grains supplies no sodium chloride, so salt has to be obtained from somewhere else. The animals that farmers raised, such as cattle, goats, sheep, and pigs, also needed to be fed salt. It is thought that wild animals were first tamed by farmers offering them salt. Soon these animals would pass their time near people in order to get the salt they needed.

Salt Preserves!

Once farmers formed communities, they began to trade and sell the things they produced. For many thousands of years, the most valued item of trade was food. But without refrigeration, food spoiled. It was discovered that salt preserved food by killing bacteria and drawing off moisture. Milk and cream could be cured with salt to become cheese. Cabbage could become sauerkraut. Cucumbers could be made into pickles. Meat could become ham or bacon, and fish could become salt fish.

Though it is unknown exactly when this was first discovered, it is one of the most significant changes in history. It meant that for the first time people could journey far from home, eating preserved food. In fact, food preserved in salt could be taken hundreds or thousands of miles away to be traded or sold.

Hence, when people had a good supply of salt, they could also have a thriving international trade, which in turn led to great power. On every continent, in every century, the dominant people were the ones who controlled the salt trade. Today, the largest producer of salt is the United States.

SALT DYNASTIES

The ancient Chinese built the first salt empire. The rulers understood the value of salt, so only the government was allowed to produce and sell it. The government could then raise the price of salt whenever they needed more money. During the Tang dynasty, which lasted from 618 to 907, half the money earned by the Chinese government came from salt.

Salt paid for the Great Wall of China, which is fifteen hundred miles long and is still standing today. It also paid for the Chinese army. But people did not like paying such high prices. Throughout Chinese history, rulers became unpopular by overcharging for salt.

SOY SAUCE

Instead of sprinkling salt on their food, the Chinese made soy sauce to get the salt they needed. To make soy sauce, they would steam fresh whole soybeans to soften them, then spread them on large straw trays. Yeast was added, and the trays were put in a dark room until mold formed on the top. Next, the beans were mixed with salt and water and stored in crock jars to ferment for up to a year. Eventually the bean mush looked like mud. The mixture was filtered through pipes and sterilized with steam, resulting in a dark, salty syrup that could be mixed with water according to taste—soy sauce!

Meals and Mummies

The Egyptians were the first to produce salted food on a large scale. The Egyptian people depended on salted fish and meat to survive when a dry year prevented crops from growing along the green banks of the Nile River. They got their salt from the African desert out past the Nile. There they found dried lake beds covered with salt that could easily be scraped up.

The ancient Egyptians saved salted food for both the living and the dead. Egyptian tombs have been found that are filled with urns of preserved foods that were meant to help the dead on their journey to the underworld.

Dead bodies were also cleaned and salted to be preserved for eternity. Without salt, there would have been no mummies.

ACROSS THE DESERT

Because salt is bulky, it is usually produced near ports or rivers to be transported by ships. But in the Sahara Desert, huge caravans of camels carried the salt. Large slabs or cone-shaped blocks of salt were wrapped in straw to travel hundreds of miles across the desert. In cities like Timbuktu, the salt would be traded for gold.

THE POWER OF A GOOD HAM

Three thousand years ago, a tribe of people called the Celts mined rock salt in central Europe. They became powerful by selling salt and salted food along the rivers of Europe. In fact, salt was so important to the Celts, they even named places for salt: One town was named Hallein, which means "saltwork," and it was near the city of Salzburg, which means "salt town."

One of the Celts' most famous products was ham, which was made by salting the thigh of a hog. The best ham was reserved for the Celts' bravest warrior, and if two warriors claimed rights to that ham, they would have to fight for it.

Even after the Celts lost control of central Europe and their salt mines were abandoned for centuries, the countries where they lived became known for their love of ham.

WELL-PRESERVED MINERS

In 1573, a strange discovery was made in the Austrian Alps. The perfectly preserved body of a man wearing bright red wool plaid clothing and a cone-shaped felt hat was found lying next to his miner's pickax. The brightness of his clothing was shocking because Europeans at that time were not known for dressing in such bright colors. Eventually, scientists concluded he was a Celtic salt miner who got trapped in a collapsed salt mine shaft around 400 B.C.— nearly 2,000 years before!

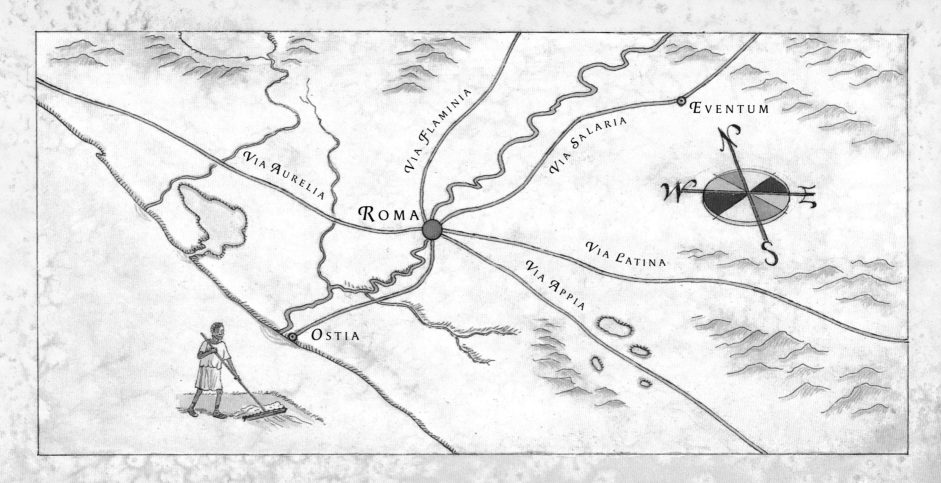

AN EMPIRE OF SALT

For centuries, the Romans ruled the Western world. And from the beginning, salt was a key to their power. Roman cities were often founded near saltworks, and one of the great Roman roads—the Via Salaria, or "salt road"—was originally built to bring salt to Rome from the nearby saltworks at Ostia.

The Romans believed that everyone had a right to salt. "Common salt" was served in a simple seashell in most households or in an ornate silver bowl at a wealthy family's feast.

Unlike the Chinese emperors, the Roman rulers did not try to own all the salt but only to control the price. To make people happy, Roman leaders tried to keep prices low. Salt was occasionally taxed to raise money for armies, but sometimes Emperor Augustus distributed free salt when he wanted to gain public support for a war.

WORDS SALTED BY THE ROMANS

Many English words are based on the Roman word for salt, *sal*—even the word "salt" itself. *Sal* is the root of the words "salary" and "soldier" because Roman soldiers were often paid in salt. This is also the origin of the expressions "worth his salt" and "to earn his salt." "Salad," too, comes from *insalata*, a salt word because Romans ate their greens with a dressing based on salt water.

Salt was central to everyday life in the Roman Empire. All along the Mediterranean Sea, Romans produced three highly valued salt products— fish sauce, purple dye, and salt fish. Many kinds of fish were cured in salt, dried, and sold throughout the Western world.

A Slightly Rotten Sauce

Would you put a sauce made from fish guts on *your* food?

The Romans made a sauce called *garum* by placing leftover fish scraps—the innards, the gills, and the tails—in earthen jars with salt until they fermented into a fishy-smelling liquid. The Romans used garum like the Chinese used soy sauce—it was added to food instead of salt. But not everyone loved garum. The naturalist Pliny said that it was rotten, and the philosopher Seneca called it an "expensive liquid of bad fish."

THE SMELL OF PURPLE

According to legend, purple dye was discovered when Hercules took his sheepdog for a walk along the sea. When the dog bit into a small shellfish called a murex, his mouth turned a strange dark color.

The Romans learned how to produce this purple dye, but it was an extremely expensive process, and only wealthy people and royalty could afford it. Julius Caesar decreed that only he and his household could wear purple-trimmed togas, and the sails of Cleopatra's ship were dyed purple.

The only problem was that the purple liquid stank. It smelled so bad that when a nineteenth-century chemist identified the purple element, it was named *bromine*, a word meaning "stench."

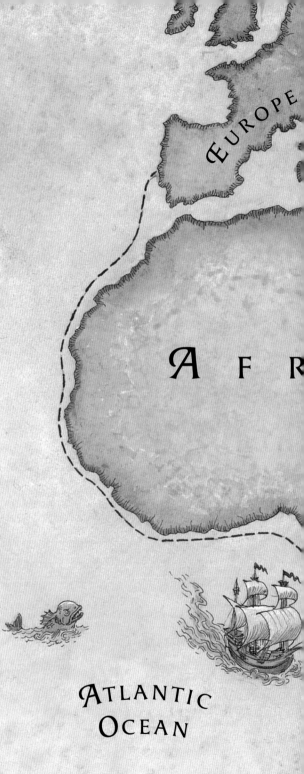

THE NEW SEA

After the fall of the Roman Empire, the Mediterranean Sea remained the center of Europe's salt trade. Two small Italian cities—Venice and Genoa—fought for centuries to control Mediterranean salt. In 1380, Venice defeated Genoa and remained dominant for a century. But then something happened.

At the time, Venetian merchants like Marco Polo would have to travel huge distances over land—eating lots of salted food along the way—to get valuable silk and spices from Asia. But in 1488, a Portuguese sea captain named Bartholomeu Dias found a faster and cheaper way to get those precious goods. He sailed from Portugal around the southern tip of Africa and into the Indian Ocean. With Dias's journey, the great age of exploration had begun.

Nations on the Atlantic Ocean such as Portugal, Spain, France, Holland, and England suddenly saw a chance to shift power from the Mediterranean Sea to their Atlantic ports. They sent out explorers like Christopher Columbus and John Cabot to the New World and greatly expanded world trade in furs and codfish—both of which had to be salted for shipping.

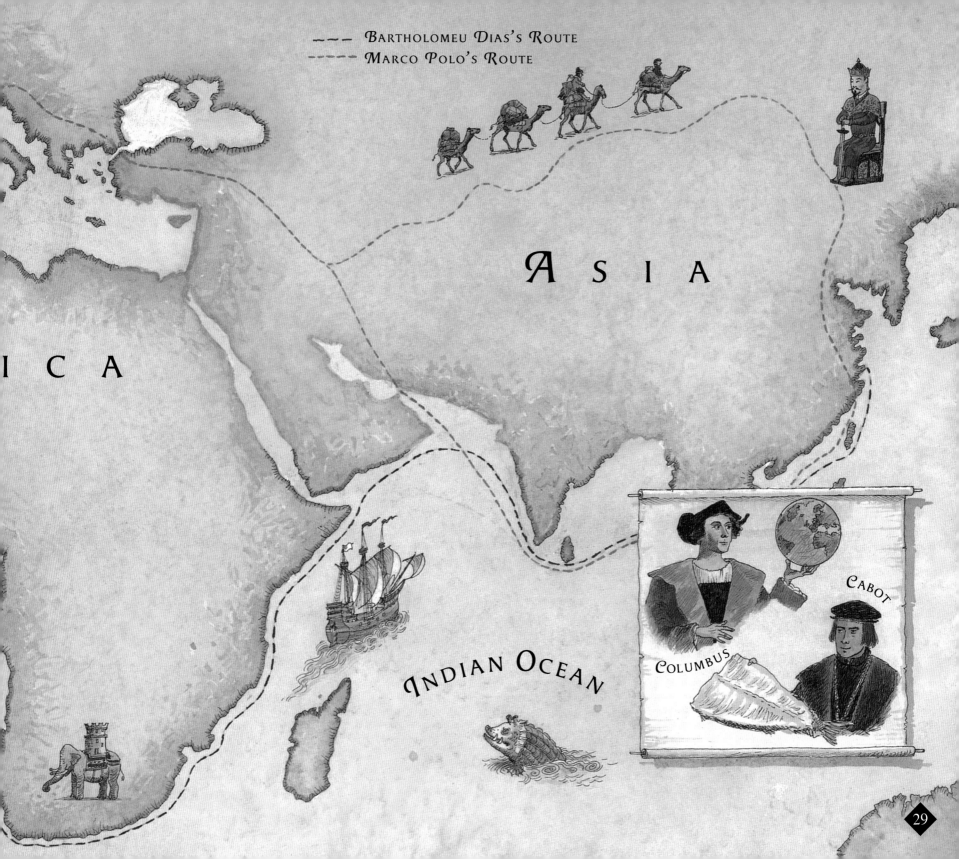

ASIA

ICA

INDIAN OCEAN

COLUMBUS

CABOT

SALT ALLIES

By the sixteenth century, northern countries like England, Holland, and those in Scandinavia were catching more and more fish for a hungry European market. In fact, from the sixteenth to the eighteenth century, sixty percent of all of the fish eaten in Europe was codfish, while much of the remaining forty percent was herring.

All of this fish needed to be cured with salt, both for taste and so that it could travel across Europe. But there was a problem: Salt was harder to get than fish!

Only southern Europe had enough sun and dry weather to make the sea salt that was ideal for salting fish. And so alliances were made and trade organizations formed between the countries with the fish and the countries with the salt. The English made a treaty with the Portuguese, and many northern countries bought salt from a German trade organization known as the Hanseatic League.

SALT AND *LIBERTÉ*

Even as the salt trade became more international, rulers still used salt to raise money in their own countries. In France, King Louis XIV raised the taxes on salt for many of his subjects. Soon enough, people began smuggling salt illegally to avoid the tax. It was smuggled across rivers at night, hidden in shipments of salt fish, and even concealed by women in their undergarments.

An entire branch of police was formed to stop salt smugglers, and by the late eighteenth century, 3,000 French men, women, and children were arrested every year for salt-related crimes—some were even sentenced to death!

THE SHIP OF STATE

The royal tables of France were set with huge ornate salt dispensers called *nefs*. *Nef* is an old French word for "ship," and these model ships were made with precious metals. The nef was always placed on the table near the king, since it was also a symbol of the "ship of state." To the French, the salt in the nef symbolized preservation and good health and that the stability of the state depended on the health of the king. The nef also sometimes contained a small drawer for an antidote to poison—helping the king to stay healthy in more than one way!

North America's Shortcoming

Before the European colonists came, the Americas followed the same pattern as other continents. The Aztecs in Mexico, the Mayans in Central America, the Incas in Peru, and the Chibcha in Colombia were all dominant civilizations who controlled the salt trade. When they lost their power, they also lost control of salt.

When the British arrived in North America, they tried to control the salt trade, too. In 1607, Captain John Smith established the colony of Jamestown in Virginia and started a saltwork. In 1660, the Dutch started a saltwork for their colony of New Amsterdam by granting the right to make salt on a small island nearby—today known as Coney Island.

New Englanders were becoming wealthy trading cod and furs while Virginia's hams were becoming famous. However, most of the salt the colonists used was bought from other British colonies in the Caribbean or directly from England's main saltwork in Liverpool.

When America declared its independence from England, their salt supply was suddenly cut off. George Washington's army lacked salt to make gunpowder, to preserve food for marches, to maintain horses, or to heal wounds. Immediately, the Continental Congress had to start paying rewards to colonists to establish saltworks, and soon America had its own salt supply.

SALTING AMERICA

After the Revolutionary War, America began to grow, and transporting salt to the new territories became a problem. So a system of canals was built, starting with the Erie Canal, which connected Lake Erie with the Hudson River. Now there was a waterway to move salt up and down the Hudson either to the Atlantic Ocean or the Great Lakes and the rapidly growing Midwest. Meatpacking became a major industry in the Midwest, and like the fisheries of the East Coast, it required huge quantities of salt.

AMERICAN ROADS

If you study a road map of anywhere in North America, it often looks as though there was no plan to the placement of towns and roads. That is because many roads are simply widened trails originally cut by animals looking for salt. People followed these trails and decided the places that had salt at the end of trails were good locations to start villages. A wide road near Lake Erie was made by buffalo, and the salt lick found at the end of it became the city of Buffalo, New York.

LICK

SALT AND SCIENCE

As modern science changed the way people lived, salt's role began to change, too. In the early nineteenth century a Frenchman named Nicolas Appert discovered that food could be preserved in airtight jars that were heated. This led to canning, which greatly decreased the market for salted fish and vegetables.

One hundred years later, Clarence Birdseye discovered how to preserve food by rapid freezing, and started a frozen food company.

At the same time, scientists had learned that salt could be broken down into the elements it was made from—sodium and chlorine. Both of these had many industrial uses. New salt-based industries were launched, including bleach, pharmaceuticals, new explosives, and bicarbonate of soda, which is used to make soft drinks.

THE SALT MARCH

While salt's economic uses changed with time, salt's symbolic power held strong. Perhaps the most famous story of salt's power was Gandhi's Salt March.

For centuries, the British had ruled India. In 1930, the Indian National Congress met to discuss ways to gain independence. A small man named Mohandas Karamchand Gandhi, who was known by the nickname Mahatma, which means "the great soul," believed that the way to popularize their cause was through salt.

At first this seemed like a peculiar idea. But Gandhi explained that the average Indian was angry because the British had banned the local manufacture of salt. They forced Indians to buy salt from Liverpool at very high prices. Not only had this left the people in salt-producing areas without a means to earn a living, but it also made salt expensive.

On March 12, 1930, Gandhi announced to Indian, British, and American newspapers that he intended to walk 240 miles to Dandi on the Arabian Sea, where he would defy British law by making salt. He started with 78 followers, but by the time he reached the Arabian Sea 25 days later, thousands had joined the march, including journalists from around the world.

With his spindly bare legs, Gandhi walked along the beach where a thick crust of salt had evaporated in the sun, and picked up a piece. Someone shouted, "Hail deliverer!" Gandhi had made salt in defiance of British law, and people celebrated throughout India. They, too, gathered salt along India's coastline and demonstrated in the cities. It was the beginning of a movement which, seventeen years later, led to Indian independence.

How Salt Lost Its Glitter

For centuries, geologists were fascinated by what were known as salt domes. While most underground salt is mined from large, shallow beds spread over a wide area, occasionally salt becomes compressed into columns that go several miles deep into the earth. The top of the dome then pushes right up to the surface, forming a slightly rounded hill with a thin layer of topsoil. Until the twentieth century, nobody knew how deep these domes went, because drills could not go very far into the earth.

In 1859, Edwin Drake was able to drill 69.5 feet on the edge of a salt dome in Titusville, Pennsylvania. Even more significantly, though geologists had said he would fail, Drake discovered oil in the dome.

Then, in 1901, Pattillo Higgins and Anthony Lucas again ignored the geologists and drilled into the edge of a salt dome in Texas known as Spindletop. A tall black fountain of oil erupted.

Scientists learned that the salt crystals in salt domes join together to form an impenetrable, glasslike wall. When other organic material gets trapped next to a dome, it slowly decomposes over millions of years and eventually turns into oil and gas.

After Spindletop, no one ever looked at salt domes or drilling the same way again. Drills and rigs became the tools of the oil industry. New drilling technology made it possible to understand what was really under the earth's surface. And soon it was discovered that salt, far from being rare, is distributed in huge beds throughout the planet.

What were once thought to be isolated salt areas were actually part of enormous underground salt deposits that stretched for thousands of miles. In the United States, one bed covers the entire Great Lakes region. Another bed begins in eastern France and goes through Germany, Austria, and southern Poland.

And so, today, when we put salt on our food, we barely give it a second thought. We live in a time when salt is taken for granted—it's common, inexpensive, and hardly worth fighting over.

But the next time you pick up a saltshaker, remember that not only do you need salt to live, you are holding rocks that shaped the history of the world!

SALT
THROUGH
THE CENTURIES

221 B.C.
China is unified for the
first time and salt becomes
a state monopoly.

52 B.C.
Julius Caesar defeats
the Celts at Alesia.

1607
Captain John Smith
establishes the colony
of Jamestown with
a saltwork.

9750 B.C.
The earliest known human
cultivation of plants—
peas, water chestnuts, and
cucumbers—in Myanmar.

264–146 B.C.
The Romans finance
Punic Wars against
Carthage with salt taxes.

A.D. 100
Natural gas is used for
the first time to boil
down the salt water of
Sichuan wells.

1380
Venice finally defeats
Genoa to dominate
Mediterranean salt trade.

6000 B.C.
Lake Yuncheng in northern
China is scraped for salt in
the dry summer months.

640 B.C.
The Romans build their
first saltwork, a seaside
pond in Ostia.

300
The first camel caravans
cross the Sahara.
Salt is one of the cargoes.

1352
Ibn Batuta, an Arab
explorer, finds a Saharan
city made entirely of salt.

2900 B.C.
The pyramid of Giza in
Egypt contains salt-preserved
mummies as well as food
offerings.

1000 B.C.
Mayans begin making
salt in Central America.

476
The fall of the
Roman Empire.

1295
Venice merchant Marco Polo
returns from China with
stories of money made from
salt and the Kublai Khan's
wealth from salt trade.

2000 B.C.
Earliest records of
Chinese preserving
fish with salt.

1300 B.C.
The beginning of a
Celtic salt-mining village
in what is today Austria.

1207
King John of England grants
permission to begin the port
of Liverpool, which will
become one of the world's
biggest salt ports.

1281
The Venetian government
starts subsidizing salt
shipments, making Venice
the salt center of
the Mediterranean.

1246
France's Louis IX establishes
Aigues Mortes saltworks to
raise money for the Crusades.

1500 B.C.
Phoenician merchants in
Tyre begin selling purple
dye from salted murex.

1800 B.C.
The Chinese begin
evaporating seawater.

1268
Austrian salt mines begin
flooding shafts with water
and pumping out brine
rather than lifting rock salt
from the mine.

46

1698

A French government official reports "salt smuggling is endless on the Loire River."

1775

The Second Continental Congress provides subsidies to American salt makers.

1776

The British take Long Island and New York, cutting off George Washington from his army's salt supply.

1787

Americans begin producing salt from underwater springs in Onondago, New York, buying the rights from the Onondago people for 150 bushels every year.

1789

The French Revolution begins, and the following year the salt taxes are abolished.

1803

Nicolas Appert sells the French navy vegetables and beef preserved through canning rather than salting, and a new industry begins.

1835

In Sichuan, China, the Shen Hai salt spring well is drilled 3,300 feet deep, the deepest well in the world until modern oil rigs.

1817

Work begins on the Erie Canal, providing a water route for Onondago salt to the Great Lakes, the Midwest, the Hudson River, and New York Harbor.

1812

The British go to war with the United States and attempt to cut off Cape Cod from supplying salt.

1807

Sir Humphrey Davy, a British chemist, isolates the element sodium, the seventh most common element on Earth, from salt, and three years later he isolates chloride. The salt-based chemical industry begins.

1804

The salt taxes are reinstated by Napoleon.

1859

Edwin Drake drills almost 70 feet in a salt dome in Titusville, Pennsylvania, and finds oil.

1859

The richest vein of silver ever discovered in the U.S., the Comstock Lode, uses salt for separating ore and drives up California salt prices.

1861

Four days after the start of the Civil War, President Lincoln orders a naval blockade of the South, stopping shipments of British salt from Liverpool from supplying the Confederacy.

1863

The British ban the local production of salt in India, forcing Indians to buy British salt shipped from Liverpool.

1901

Pattillo Higgins and Anthony Lucas drill the Spindletop salt dome in Texas and so much oil gushes out that the age of petroleum begins.

1947

India gains its independence from Britain and becomes a major salt producer.

1946

French salt taxes finally end.

1930

Gandhi leads a 240-mile march to the sea to make salt, defying the British ban.

1925

Clarence Birdseye moves to the fishing port of Gloucester and begins fast-freezing rather than salting cod, beginning the frozen-food industry.

1924

The Morton Salt Company, at the request of the Michigan medical association, adds iodine to its salt. Iodized salt has become the leading tool in fighting iodine deficiency around the world.

For Talia Feiga —M.K.

To Leslie Talon —S.D.S.

PUFFIN BOOKS
Published by the Penguin Group
Penguin Group (USA) LLC
375 Hudson Street
New York, New York 10014

USA * Canada * UK * Ireland * Australia
New Zealand * India * South Africa * China

penguin.com
A Penguin Random House Company

First published in the United States of America by G. P. Putnam's Sons,
a division of Penguin Young Readers Group, 2006
Published by Puffin Books, an imprint of Penguin Young Readers Group, 2014

THE LIBRARY OF CONGRESS HAS CATALOGED THE G. P. PUTNAM'S SONS EDITION AS FOLLOWS:
Kurlansky, Mark. The story of salt / by Mark Kurlansky ; illustrated by S. D. Schindler.
p. cm.
ISBN 0-399-23998-7 (hardcover)
1. Salt—Popular works. 2. Salt—History—Popular works. 3. Salt industry and trade—History—Popular works.
I. Title. TN900.K866 2006 553.6'3209—dc22 2005032629

Puffin Books ISBN 978-0-14-751166-9

10

Manufactured in China